Outlandish

Damian Le Bas and Jo Clement
Illustrated by W. John Hewitt

First published 2019 by New Writing North

Paperback ISBN 978-0-9930588-3-7

Cover design by New Writing North

Cover illustration by W. John Hewitt

Printed and bound by CPI colour

New Writing North
Ellison Terrace, Newcastle, Tyne and Wear, NE1 8ST
www.newwritingnorth.com

Outlandish was commissioned by Durham Book Festival in 2019

Acknowledgements

Many thanks to Claire and Rebecca at New Writing North for suggesting we work on something, which has turned into *Outlandish*. Thanks to Jude for the design of this book, to Carol Gorner and the Gordon Burn Trust, and to the people we met and talked to whilst walking. Thanks to Arts Council England for supporting this project, and our friends and families for supporting us.

Contents

Every day is a journey,
and the journey itself is home.
Matsuo Bashō

my eyes were in my feet
Nan Shepherd

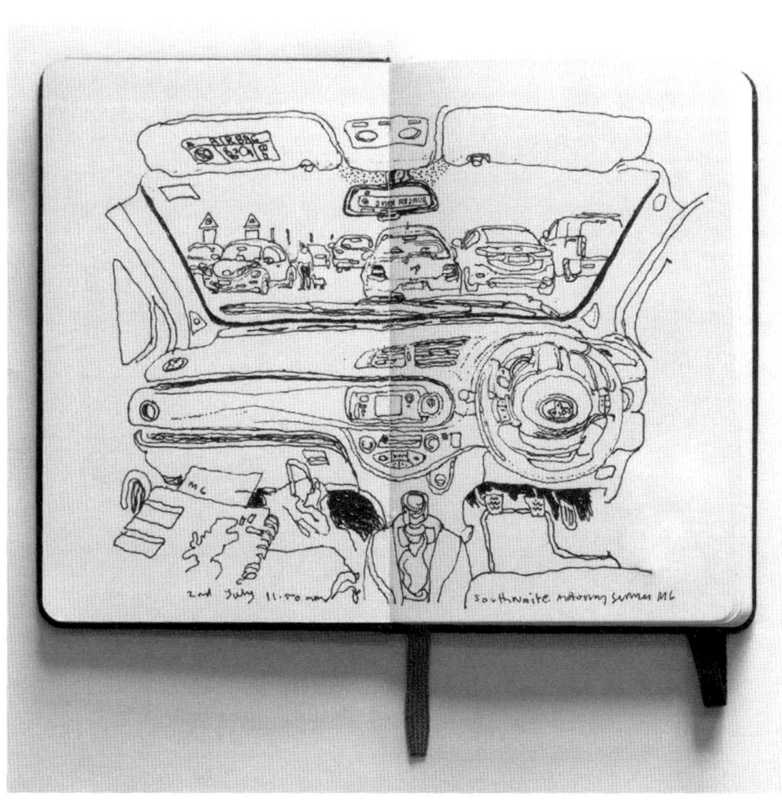

AIRBAG
2nd July 11.50 am
Southwaite motorway services M6

Crown

These are the standing stones,
and what feet they have known,

to crown Yetholm's Kings
and Queens. No plaque marks

the place, they define themselves
keeping oaths given to the wind,

smoked peat-blue as turf
that knew no border. Off and on,

they'd take your ears
for using the wrong tongue,

so we held them dear
as bairns to the breast,

sharp as ground knives.
At Stob Stane, Spey has me

by the throat, as I step up
to hear the Common.

Melrose Roofers

Walking this close to the vertical
gives the old job a faint touch of the miracle:
climbers might claw up an incline like this
but we step up them, burdened,
shore safety one-handed.

Foot that ladder, pal! Jesus!
I saw Dougal Armstrong rock twice in a crosswind,
his stairway unanchored
by a mate's ballast.
He fell limbs-out, a stiff angel.
I'll never forget the dull punch
on the earth where he landed.

A mason at graft
in the Abbey's ghost rafters
unshelved a pink capstone
that wore my initials.
An ancestor, maybe,
trussed high in a sling
with a pouch and three chisels
to work the implacable.
Eight hundred years
that stone laid, underwritten.
I guarantee my work for ten.

This morning a wee laddie here
on a scheme for offenders
looked up toward heaven
and jiggled his ladder,
its edges drumkissing the guttering
where dust is washed
from the scales of dwelling.

I signed his placement off
like the climbing cost of life:

it's a bit steep, son,
but it's all right.

Travellers

i.

We snubbed the bald coasts
so the land was endless:
wide as we wanted
while wed to our circles.

Each roadside fire
each cup of *char*
was a lit rebellion
of life over laws' blather.

We knew castles' heft
for a songbirds' keep
while our light bowcamp
with its slick tarp
was the breathing home
with the working hearth.

ii.

Pickled in history, bigwigs ignored us:
how we struck sunsetward for Appleby
or zigzagged up to the Spey,
saw jackdaws peer into pools like priests
and flung up sung confetti, *Dordi dordi!*

'Gypsy' then was a step-stopping clanger
a hinged heartbeat, something caught in the zipper.

'Travellers' sounded like notes to a future
continents' cusps uncrystallised
our race cutting more than a curt question.

iii.

Now sagged cheeks glow with stowed spirits
bursting for a full blether
from fear of a heatherless hereafter,

and old that I am,
I can frame my mistake
when I thought old men simply stared at the ground,

for the truth lies halfway between eyes and earth
at the vanishing point of the chance to change,
which is therefore also the perfect range
for watching the old fire burning.

At Eildon

Hard into heels, we found ourselves
walking to rise with the Sisters,

the van ever below, safe as houses.
Trusted with distance, you steady the pack

cinching my collar, that pulled me back.
Steep, the old way knew what lived in there,

pressing as a lurcher kneels onto a hare,
brindles its curve into the snow's unrest.

It saw the clearing in a black wood
and a lass behind the lamp,

who looks as I did then, heather-scuffed,
overstepping fizzy wires,

slicing light onto birch backs,
her boots, steel signs. Eildon knows our stake,

Hawkers, Moonmen, Gypsies,
names we tried to hide. Out of Scott's view,

we sit a spell in the saddle
to unshoulder its writhe.

Every stitch read *Trespass,*
I couldn't leave it behind.

Buster at the Playing Stone 2.45 on 3rd July with good finish + crow

Wild Camp

To hell with the abbey,
we found a place between the pebbles —

> *look, a heron by the edges, peripheral*
> *flies over —*

so here we are, bivvied by the Tweed like two rocks
and yeah, I suppose the patriarchy won't have fucked off

until we can stop talking about *man hours, stag dos*
and my pay matches yours —

> *see the angler making his way down?*
> *He's rivered to his thighs,*
> *a shadow casting out lines into the darkness,*
> *the fish jumping for flies —*

or perhaps it's when we no longer need to explain
how two people might walk, talk and sleep together

like this without any such complication

> or even write
a poem without a Gypsy in it, oh no it's too late —

> *listen, the birds are dying off —*

Heron

Over thresholds of nothing
her slow hurdling

arcs the moment,
spans potentials.

She body-pops,
stops,

crouches into a slow wedge
at the river's blatting edge.

Poised, full of herself, hinged
she rears now, and unlatches

stealth into shot
and catches.

Kirk Yetholm ragged school 4 July 2·50 pm

After Flodden

Lager cans' fallen pillars
lay by bracken's curled triggers,

hollow fates sealed
when their wet weight spilled

by cut straw, massed
in fat gold reels

on earth baked to cracks.
Fell ponies dip profiles

in veils of light.
Tall trees remain ramrod

before truant wind,
and kestrels bob

on an absence of storm:
a faked obeisance.

Conifers – earth's hairs –
stand stock straight

by rubber-polished roads
where hedgehogs burst

to blown berries
and rabbits split, twisted,

detached tails flagging
on cold crosswinds

that drop nude-necked thrushes
on punitive litterpicks.

This bracken has learned
the dry swoon of cars:

it reiterates them,
long husks of prayers,

while the elderly beech
stands whispering witness.

Song of a Yetholm Queen

Living light is for butterflies.
The old folk dressed as such:

furs flanking the abdomen,
painted parts to reel glances like fishes

and wings of survivors' arrogance
to flap to futures with stuffed purses.

Such is the story. I balk at its purity,
breathing the sky and derived from my mother.

Bemused to discover my skin bought controversy
free of deliberate feint at transaction,

I knelt before no one. I scrutinised Scotland,
measured my steps from the dawn to the payment

strewn in my palm like the seed of a parable
falling with speed that adjusted for willingness.

I was taught well how life lurches to bitterness;
how a sin sown in the wild may sprout

in the city, where judges' jaws snap like the guillotines.
Heir to cautions, I keep tales of a sentence:

mind bailiffs, they'll confiscate necklace and cattle.
*They hanged five in Durham for being our kind.**

So, settled as much as I'm tented in bricks –
a cast state, far-fetched, curiosity

I pack out my mindshelves with bloodbooks and kinsongs
and feel in the back muscles running by spine-side

the strength of hillranges like backs of old goddesses
ridged like beast backbones and notched like the Eildons.

My window lets light like the windows of wagons
or boats beached in yards, resting miles from seaways,

and down to my nest of old age, deed and costliness
swallows and bats bring their looplines of tidings

that tell of the quiets that follow the cryings
that follow the hidings that follow the ridings.

* In August 1592 five persons 'counterfeiting themselves to be
Egyptians' were condemned to the gallows at Durham.

Cessford

In this debatable land what is it in us
that builds a doorless house
with twelve feet of bricks
and a ladder pulled up behind?

·

Welcome to
KIRK YETHOLM
Please drive carefully
4 July 4·00 pm   the Gypsy palace on the hill

Paisley

With India's hand on the loom,
I untwist a paisley square

from round my neck:
red, green and gold

threads repeat almonds
some call figs, figs the Welsh

call pears and pears you might
call teardrops. Shook onto

the grass, I smooth out Kashmir
— so close to silk —

over the fault line made
of my body: feet in England,

head in Scotland,
a heart elsewhere.

SLOW
5 July 1.00pm
westwood bridge

Outlandish

Conied in scraps, her Meg is cast,
    creeks oak-slow and ashen

hoyed men at floodlights
    lifting the hot glare of lint.

This seer, this Sibyl, burst flax to flames,
    tore her voice to rags. The papers

coined her a foreign familiar:
    the *Gypsiness* of weird women,

pythons, queens. Tell us, Cushman,
    how the curtain skimmed your ankle,

sounding that inner applause
    that you can take off the dress.

Charlotte Cushman played the character of Meg Merrilies in transatlantic theatrical adaptations of Walter Scott's *Guy Mannering* (1815). Meg is described by Scott as a 'harlot, thief, witch and gipsy'.

For William Waller, shoemaker of Newcastle-upon-Tyne

I have cried for my God
as I cried for my mother

I have moulded the leather
as winds smoor the heather

I have clung to my wife
as the flag to the staff

I have footed the road
as the king and the horse

I found company out
with the masterless men

I glimpsed bravery there
in the woodsmoke and shades

and was seized like a purse
by the thugs of the rules

and confessed to the judge
That I'd cobbled offence

and perhaps I had asked
if I'd harboured the courage

how fake pharaoh-taint
makes a cloak of defence

In 1618 Waller confessed he had travelled 'under the pretence of a counterfeit Egyptian, and at Ashton under Lyme had met up with his wife and child and divers other strangers, who also travelled as counterfeit Egyptians'.

A Riding, with Tent

I trot softly
in swinging stirrups

past lonesome towers
of gormless strength

backed to the hilt
by the stoical forest.

The landscape's cracked mirror
bounds off out of kilter

and the Chillingham bull
blows its relict bellow

while the frail rod tent
shoulders storms:

a flutterskinned ribcage
muzzling hardship.

CHRIS
E LISA
Y1818
DAVID
DOUGLES
JoANNEC
2019
F.W.
T.A
1852

Family Silver

Let me sing of my greatest
grandfather's knife. He graved

the tooth with scrimshaw cobs,
so he might remember to handle

the blade as gently as his horses.
Kept it sharp enough to gut a trout,

split a clutch of pegs. Sharper
still to cross palms with silver,

he called it *churi*, sweet talked maids
between their lady's petticoats.

How strange those fingers
might squeeze a noble waist.

Left on the grass,
an open wooden hand.

Lindisfarne Path

Twice daily flayed
to a cellulite desert,

these flats where fly language
blows in a blether

to a barnacled Alhambra
of worm-shot manuscripts

and the skew-whiff traces
of life by salt government:

ropes of crab skeletons,
wreaths of dry reedskins,

winkleshell sandbanks
and wormcast-built ridges.

Phone signal lapses.
The whole map turns grey,

a land lost in fog
of a satellite's yaw.

Imagine a book
where the pages blink absent,

time's weary fug
seived into a stammer

across clootie wetland
of sea-gummed ages.

These stilted huts
are flimsy pele towers

for hapless scarperers
under scrapes of cloud.

The wind works away
at these bubble wrap ruins,

corrective beatings,
patient polishing,

while aggressionless birdsong
dances under high arches

and hushed Christians
palm prayers and currency.

*This wine is my blood
and this bread is my body,*

bread wanting violence
for its staged birthings:

a torturer's process
of beatings and brandings.

Without these indignities
grains are chewed fruitlessly.

So Cuthbert found
on the land's buckled slope

to his cave's blunt mouth
with its mouldering sheen

where the damp devils
made polite suggestions

that he command these wheatears
to be fit for digestion.

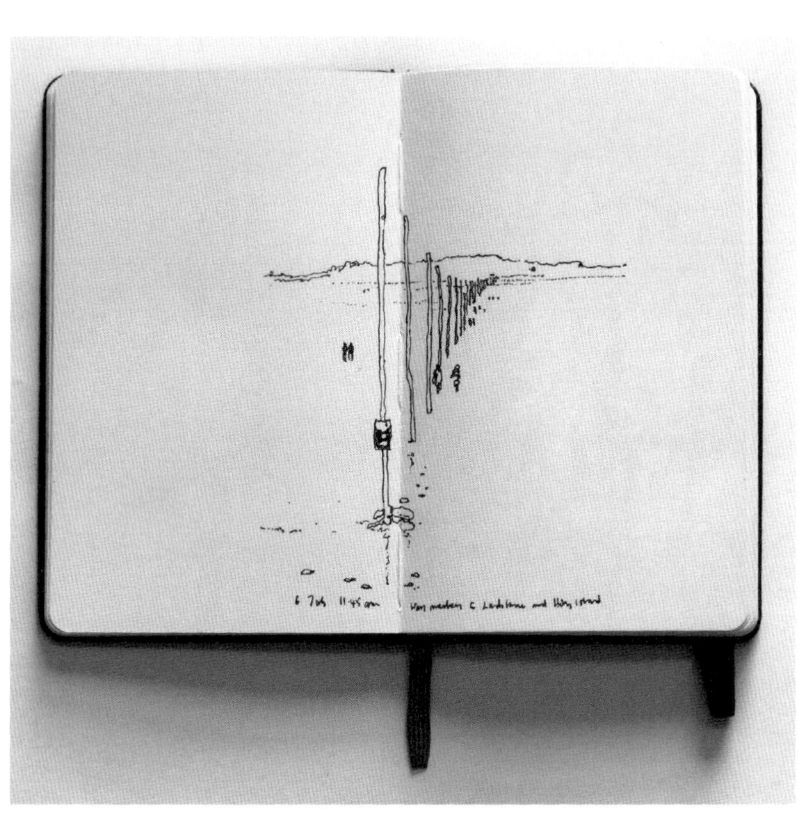

6 July 11.45 am   Ham markers G Lindisfarne and Holy Island

A Wonderful Fish

A fish in the mouth of a silver swan
is eaten endlessly. Beak closed,

he holds it under his tongue,
until the show of clockwork lets it play.

A fish moth sits under my tongue, too,
born between the pages of a glued

paper house. Such a small fish,
silvered, it lives between my teeth,

swimming in the slaver, tickling
its way to speak of our lost *vardo*,

the sulky horse. Of silk scarves it might
make holes in, of books it might

make homes in. For the fish who can eat
the binding, can eat *The Bible*.

Periwinkle

You speak from this edge and colour
the impossible grey, who for once,

holds its breath as you dare to be
so yellow and small, smaller

and more yellow than anything
to ever find this shore. In the eye

of your whorl I see them slipping,
picking cockles at night, fighting

the tide. Not of this sea but that one,
though I don't know how or why

they map a difference. It's all salt.
There is a delicacy and a hardness

to shell, as slight and hollow
as the moment you hear the words

illegal immigrant missing
change to *human skull found.*

Causeway

We're glad of what we're given
and so because we must, we walk

between places, our boots shiny
as seal pups. Earlier a crab,

a hot jar of honey. On the island,
I saw swifts flute the ruined chimney,

they'll be in Africa by now.
The sea, always arriving.

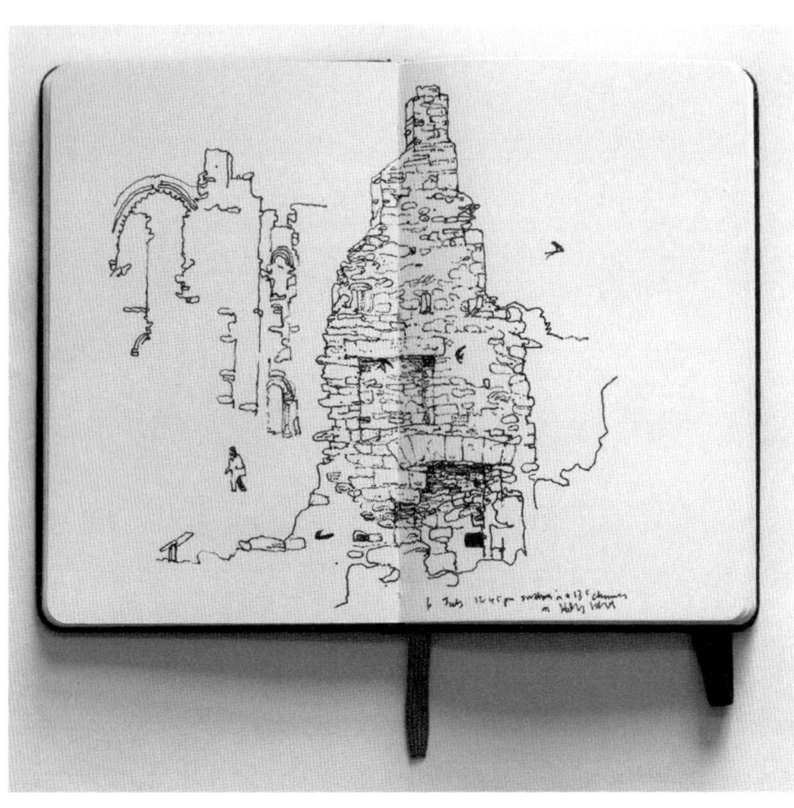

6 July 3·35pm The rear view in Donnie Leba's van

6 June 3.15 pm   Damian Dallas' Ford transit

Sod's Law

When I got my first truck
they declared fumes fatal,
fire-fed speed sinful,

as if to bolt the door
on our fresh-freed spirit
a thousand years stabled.

I swung back, swearing
I'd slung my sods,
and I'd drive by the laws

of my given gods:
hunger, and hawking
for evener odds.

Woman Encamped, with View of City Walls

In Durham's still towers
I see clay pipes upended,
stone in swung circles,
rock to bend roads round
and a soft dread distended.

Do towers dispense ash
from dungeons' dead linings
like the tiny grey castles
Nan tapped from her pipe
under black winds' whinings?

In the rain's frantic race
down canyoned dark stone
I see water's pitiless pace
down the defensive architecture
of her backbone and face.

Biographies

Damian Le Bas is a writer and occasional filmmaker. His first book, *The Stopping Places: a Journey through Gypsy Britain*, was published by Chatto & Windus in 2018. It won the Somerset Maugham Award, the Jerwood Award, was BBC Radio 4 Book of the Week, and was shortlisted for the Stanford Dolman Travel Book of the Year.

Dr Jo Clement received a New Writing North Award in 2012, selected by Paul Farley. Her poems have been shortlisted for the Bridport, Melita Hume and Troubadour International prizes. Jo holds a practice-led PhD in Creative Writing from Newcastle University, which was awarded an inaugural AHRC Northern Bridge scholarship. She is Managing Editor of *Butcher's Dog* poetry magazine. joclement.co.uk

Dr John Hewitt is a printmaker and daily drawer. His artworks are housed in collections including the V&A, the Museum of London and the Government Art Collection. He completed a PhD on drawing and memory in 2008. John is an Honorary Fellow of the Royal College of Art and was awarded the Hugh Casson Prize for Drawing at the Royal Academy Summer Exhibition in 2016.